Things We're Pretty Sure They Said about the Author:

I am looking forward to Glenn being in the fifth grade!

Glenn's fourth grade teacher

He is one of those challenges that makes a teacher think about a real estate career.

Assistant Principal, Emerson School

Glenn is a wonderful little boy, who is a joy to all who meet him.

His mother

He has given me incentive to study hard and get a scholarship to private school.

Snobby Donna

Glenn is a very loud singer. His parents should take him to Hollywood or New York or Somerville.

Mr. McDonald, his neighbor

He is the cutest boy in class. I should have danced with him.

The little blond-haired girl

A Boy's First Diary

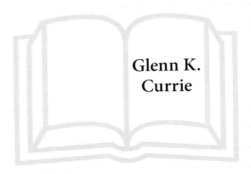

Glenn K.
Currie

Snap Screen Press

CONCORD, NEW HAMPSHIRE

ISBN 978-0-9779675-1-3
Library of Congress Control Number: 2007900657

Designed and composed in Adobe Minion Pro at
Hobblebush Books, Brookline, New Hampshire
www.hobblebush.com

Printed in the United States of America

Published by:
SNAP SCREEN PRESS
6 Dwinell Drive
Concord, NH 03301

For more information, visit the website at:
www.snapscreenpress.com
or e-mail:
GlennKC@aol.com

Contents

Letter to the Editor

My teacher said I had to send this to you.
She's always giving me extra homework.
I think she's mad at me
'Cause I hit Snobby Donna with a water balloon.

This was supposed to be a secret diary,
But Billy took it from my desk,
And then Snobby Donna told Miss Barry
That we were fighting in the hall.

I'm not sure what an editor does.
Do you work for the principal's office?
If so, it wasn't me who put the gum in his lock.
Billy and I were up on Cedar Avenue then.

When you send this book back,
Please make sure you send it directly to me.
I don't want my Mom and Dad to see it,
Or I'll be eating turnip for a month.

Sincerely,

Master Glenn K. Currie

Master Glenn K. Currie

ix

Introduction

These little poems have been in a dark, dusty place in the corner of my mind for the last fifty-two years. They have finally seen the light of day only because I have been assured that the statute of limitations has run out, and my mother won't ground me.

My apologies to all the people mentioned. Some are real people and some are combinations of several childhood friends, blended together for simplicity. All of the stories are pretty much true, although, as with most ten or eleven-year-old boys, there may have been some embellishment.

To those of you who think they recognize themselves in these poems and are displeased: be assured that it is not you. That character is purely fictional. To those of you who remember the events favorably, thanks for sharing my childhood.

The places in Stoneham, Massachusetts, were all real at one time, but many have since disappeared, worn away by time. There are, however, many remnants still there, for those who wish to search them out.

The Christmas Tree War

We had a Christmas tree war this week.
Wendell and his cousins made a fort
From Christmas trees that people put out.
They attacked us after school.

It was a really good fort.
Drooley got a slushball right in the face.
Early Saturday morning
We snuck over and grabbed their trees.

We made an even better fort
At the top of the hill,
Behind my house.
We made a lot of snowballs.

Billy and Drooley and I were ready.
Wendell figured it was us.
They attacked Saturday afternoon.
It was a great snowball fight.

Then Mom came out and stopped it.
She made everyone go home.
Then she told us to bring the trees back
Where they came from.

We didn't know where that was.
We decided to wait until dark,
And dump them in Mr. Seibert's yard.
My dad says his yard is a dump.

Saturday Matinee

Today was not a good day.
The old guy at the movies
Made our whole row leave.
And we didn't get our money back.

He said we were throwing stuff.
The kids in back started it.
They were throwing popcorn,
And making burping noises.

I didn't throw any popcorn.
I maybe threw a couple of Jujubes.
Billy said if you wet them
They would stick to the screen.

The kids in back were the troublemakers.
We only blew on our drink straws
And played tunes on the Junior Mint boxes.
Everybody does that.

We missed half the matinee,
And I wasted most of my candy.
I didn't even have any popcorn.
Billy was right about the Jujubes.

Turnip

Mom sure was mad.
We were playing with our food.
We didn't like the turnip.
Except to make faces in it.

It looked like old swamp mud
And it had little lumps in it.
Mom said we had to eat it.
We didn't want to eat swamp mud.

She made us sit at the table
For a very long time.
Mom and Dad went to watch TV.
I put some turnip down the sink.

My sister didn't even tell,
She doesn't like turnip either.
It was cold and hard.
And it smelled like Billy's shoes.

We never did eat the turnip.
We were sent to bed.
Mom was really mad.
This morning the sink was clogged.

Snow Days

We didn't have any school today.
It was snowing really hard.
We made snowmen and snow angels.
Then we came in to get warm.

Then we went out to slide.
We have the best sliding hill ever,
Until the sand truck comes.
Cars stay away from the hill until then.

We post lookouts and sometimes go
From the top of Cedar Ave. to Montvale.
After lunch we went out again.
Then we came in to warm up.

Mom said that was enough in and out.
We were running out of clothes.
I put my mittens on the radiator.
They got all crispy and smelled funny.

If it's still snowing tomorrow,
We'll build a snow fort.
Mom says God forbid
It should snow tomorrow.

I guess they had a chat.

Dike's Wall is where we build our snow forts.
Our sliding hill goes all the way to Montvale.

My Little Sister

My little sister is a pain.
She's always following me.
She copies what I do,
And tells Mom on me.

One time I gave her a haircut;
It looked pretty.
Mom was really mad;
I got in a lot of trouble.

Another time Billy and I built a tree house.
She said she would tell
If we didn't let her come up.
Then she was afraid to come down.

I had to go get Dad.
He brought a big ladder,
And climbed up to get her.
I got in a lot of trouble.

Sometimes we play together
And she's okay.
But whenever we do bad stuff,
I always get blamed.

Aunt May

Sometimes I help Aunt May.
She lives alone in a big house.
I help her feed the birds.
She's really old. Even Mom says so.

She's not really my aunt.
But she's nice. She smells like lilacs.
She comes to our house
For Thanksgiving and Christmas.

Aunt May is upset at the squirrels.
They always get the birds' food.
Yesterday, we put up a new feeder
That squirrels can't get to.

We put a lot of suet and seed in it.
Aunt May likes the chickadees.
Today when I visited,
Two squirrels were eating the seeds.

Besides playing goalie,
the other bad thing about pond hockey
is that the big kids hog the puck.

Pond Hockey

Some days, after school,
We play hockey at Dike's Pond.
The last guy picked,
Always has to play goalie.

I always get picked last.
I don't have good skates.
They're my uncle's old skates,
And they don't attach to my shoes right.

Johnny is the best player.
Yesterday he got a breakaway on me.
I got nervous and fell down
Just when he shot.

I stopped the puck with my face,
And got a bloody nose.
Billy said some brains leaked out,
But it was just nose snot.

When I got home,
Dad said I should use the stick
To stop the puck.
I don't like being goalie.

Snow Bombing

Billy and I built a snow fort,
Up on top of Dike's wall.
We wait for trucks to come up the hill.
Then we drop snow bombs on them.

Snow bombs are like super snowballs.
We throw them down in the back of trucks.
They go real slow at the top of the hill.
They make easy targets.

The drivers can't stop on the hill,
Or they have to back all the way down.
They open their window and wave.
They think we're number 1.

Today, a dump truck stopped after the hill.
Two big guys started walking back.
Billy and I abandoned the fort.
We hid up behind Aunt May's house.

When we came back,
They had destroyed the fort.
We got mad and pushed all the snow,
Down into the street.

The next two trucks
Got stuck at the top,
And had to back all the way down.
Then Billy's Dad got stuck.

We decided to go play at Drooley's.

Sliding

I like sliding.
We take our snow dishes
To the golf course.
They have big hills.

The only problem with dishes is
You can't steer them.
If a big tree is coming
You have to fall off.

Snow gets down your shirt
And in your pants.
It gets very cold and wet.
And your mittens freeze up.

There are no bathrooms at the golf course.
Mom says she can tell
When I have been sliding too long.
She says I run funny.

Today, I didn't run funny.
I made it all afternoon.
And the snow down my pants
Wasn't as cold.

Ice Cream

The Hood man left some milk
While we were in New Hampshire.
It was really cold out.
The milk bottles popped their tops.

The cream was sticking out the top
Like a naked banana.
The milk caps were still on the ends.
Dad said it was ice cream.

I don't like the cream.
We usually pour it off,
And Dad eats it with cereal.
But there are always pieces floating around.

Billy's mom gets homogenized milk.
There aren't any yellow chunks in it.
I told Mom we should get that too.
We shouldn't have to chew our milk.

The Opera

Last night Mom took me to opera.
She has community theater tickets.
There were a lot of old people there.
They didn't smile much.

The singers wore funny costumes.
They couldn't sing in English.
I didn't know what was happening.
But a guy died for a long time.

Halfway through, the show stopped.
I guess everyone needed a break.
I know I did. I got a box of Pom Poms.
Intermission was the best part.

My sister was lucky.
She didn't have to come.
At the end, the curtain closed a lot,
But the singers wouldn't go away.

Singing

I got picked to sing on the radio.
It was the newsboys' show.
I was in the newspaper.
And I got paid 50 cents a show.

Mom had to take me to Boston
Early on Saturday mornings.
We went on the bus and train.
It cost more than 50 cents.

After two trips, we got tired.
Mom said we couldn't afford it.
It was fine with me.
Billy and I play on Saturdays.

Last Friday I sang for a big crowd
At the town hall assembly.
I sang "America the Beautiful,"
But I didn't get 50 cents.

Mickey Mouse

Yesterday, Dad caught a mouse
In our basement,
Behind the furnace.
The trap caught his tail.

We all went to see him.
He was really cute.
He looked just like Mickey.
My sister thought so too.

We told Dad he couldn't kill Mickey.
But Dad was mad at Mickey.
He took him outside. Mom was mad too.
He said he let him go, but I'm not sure.

Billy said regular mice don't look like Mickey.
So this must have been Mickey.
Dad could get in a lot of trouble
For killing Mickey Mouse.

So far, it's not in the papers.

The Test

Miss Baker made me change seats.
Now I'm sitting with all girls.
She says it's 'cause of the tests I took.
Something I did like eighth graders.

Mom says I'm in a special group,
That I'm really lucky.
Snobby Donna is sitting next to me;
I don't feel so lucky.

I'm stuck with all the girls;
I have to read extra, boring stuff.
There's a lot more homework
And the kids think I'm teacher's pet.

Billy was smarter.
He filled in all "d's" on the test.
Then he went out to recess
Until everyone else was finished.

Billy doesn't get as much homework.

Prayers

I make up my own prayers now.
I'm bigger and God understands me.
He did before, too,
But I didn't understand him.

Prayers are a little scary.
I sort of know what they mean,
But as I fall asleep
I sometimes worry about them.

"If I should die before I wake,
 I pray the Lord my soul to take . . ."
I always add an extra prayer,
Not to die before I wake.

"Shirley, goodness and mercy shall follow me
 All the days of my life . . ."
 I wonder about who Shirley is,
 And why she is following me.

"The Lord is my shepherd,
 I shall not want . . ."
Actually, I do want God
 To watch over me.

I like my own prayers better.

The Flower Show

Mom made us all go to the flower show.
We got stuck in a lot of traffic.
Dad doesn't like traffic.
My sister got carsick.

It was in a big building in Boston.
Inside was a huge garden.
There were lots of old ladies there.
It smelled like Aunt May's perfume.

We walked and walked and walked.
After a while, Dad carried my sister.
I got lost in the shrub section.
I almost cried. Then Mom found me.

We had seen enough flowers.
Then Dad couldn't find the car.
It was a big garage.
Dad was on the wrong floor.

On the way home,
We got stuck in traffic again.
My sister got carsick again.
I learned some new words.

Piano Lessons

Mom is making me take piano lessons.
Mr. Davies says I have to practice,
At least a half-hour a day.
The songs are really boring.

None of the songs have words.
They're written by guys named Mozart and Beethoven.
Who names their kids that?
No wonder they stayed indoors by the piano.

They should let us play popular music.
Nobody dances to minuets.
All those classical guys are dead,
And they were bad dressers, too.

I told Mom it wasn't fair.
How come my sister doesn't take lessons.
Now she has to practice too.
I feel a little better.

The Substitute Teacher

We had a substitute teacher today.
Her name was Miss Dawson.
Usually we like substitutes.
They just sit up there and read.

Butchy said we should all change seats.
She didn't know who anybody was.
Then Butchy, Billy and I
Snuck out the back to play games.

Snobby Donna ratted us out.
And we all went back to regular seats.
Miss Dawson was pretty upset.
She had to redo the whole attendance list.

Then Henry started fanny burping.
Henry always sits in the back.
Nobody sits next to him.
His family eats beans for breakfast.

Pretty soon we all started making noises,
Except for Snobby Donna.
Then Mr. Mullins came in
And said we couldn't have recess cookies.

They were our favorites today,
The sugar wafers.
Snobby Donna got four.
Everybody is mad at Henry.

Saturday Morning

I got up really early Saturday.
A bird was singing at my window.
I think it was an oriole.
The sun was shining in my face.

Mom and Dad were still asleep.
I went out to play in the yard.
All the flowers were coming up.
Violets were all over the hill.

All of a sudden, I don't know why,
I just started singing as loud as I could.
I sang "Oh What a Beautiful Morning."
I can sing pretty loud.

I walked down Hersam to Wright Street,
And I kept singing.
The trees were new green,
The sun was dancing in the long shadows.

I woke up the whole neighborhood.
They should enjoy the morning too.
Mr. McDonald stared out his window.
I don't think he likes mornings.

Mrs. Buck called my mom.
She said I sang really good.
Mom said six o'clock was a little early,
For a Saturday morning.

Try Outs

I tried out for Little League,
But my glove was too small.
It was my uncle's when he was little.
It didn't catch that good.

The other kids laughed at it.
They had new big gloves.
Their gloves caught better.
No one played catch with me.

I hit the ball okay,
But I didn't get picked.
They said I was too small.
I think it was my glove.

They sent me to farm league,
Where no one could catch
Even with the big gloves.
I got a hat with a "D."

I like farm league.
They don't care if I'm little,
Or that my glove is little.
I wish they gave us uniforms.

The Blond-Haired Girl

Sometimes I used to play
With a blond-haired girl
Who lived down the street.
Her name is Mary Jane.

She had a playhouse
And we would pretend to have tea.
I thought she was nice, for a girl.
I liked when she smiled.

Last week we had dance class.
They made us dance with girls.
I asked her to dance with me,
But she said I was too short.

I had to dance with Mrs. Hess.
I was pretty embarrassed.
Billy was right about girls,
He says you can only trust puppies.

Dancing with Mrs. Hess

After Mary Jane said I was too short,
I got stuck dancing with Mrs. Hess.
Mrs. Hess is really big.
I couldn't reach very far around her.

My head barely came up above her waist.
Her chest was hitting me in the face.
She was wearing some boney thing
And I got injured during the fox trot.

I got poked in the left eye.
It only hurt for a few minutes.
I can see out of it okay now.
It didn't get swelled up.

Billy said I was really lucky.
I could have been crushed to death,
Or maybe suffocated
If we had fallen down.

Playing Catch

I don't think Dad likes to play catch.
He says I always ask him when he's working.
If I ask enough times, he says okay.
But then we just go out in the street.

I always have to stand on the downhill end.
Dad says it's because I throw bad.
But then when I don't catch the ball,
Sometimes it rolls all the way down to Montvale.

Our games of catch don't last long.
After three or four times running down the hill
I'm ready for a break and we stop.
Dad just sits on the porch while I chase it.

I think Dad should stand at the downhill end.
Mom says he needs more exercise.
Chasing the ball down to Montvale is good exercise.
I wouldn't need a break if I sat on the porch.

The Elephant Tree

There's a really big tree
On the top of Ted's hill.
Its bark is like elephant skin.
The branches are low, good for climbing.

We like to swing on the branches
And play tree tag.
Becky only goes halfway up,
But Billy and I go to the top.

The top is higher than Mr. Schulz's house.
You can see Main Street.
One time at the top, I slipped.
I caught a branch lower down.

I don't think Mom knows
About the elephant tree.
But Becky's mom saw us today.
She made Becky go home.

She wrote down our phone numbers.
I might have mixed up a number.
Billy gave her Wally's number.
I think Wally is in a lot of trouble.

Dad says every time an elephant dies,
an elephant tree grows.
Of course he also says every time a frog croaks,
we get rabbits.
Dad's a little strange sometimes.

Father's Day

Roxie and I made toast for Dad.
It was Father's Day.
He always says he likes burnt toast,
So we cooked it twice for him.

Then we snuck into his room
And jumped on him and Mom.
They were really surprised.
It's a good way to wake him up.

While we were jumping on him,
I saw a round balloon thing,
Sitting on the night table.
Roxie and I tried to blow it up.

We asked him what it was for.
Dad said it was for his injured toe.
An injured toe on Father's Day is bad.
It's a good thing we came to cheer him up.

Dad really liked the burnt toast.
He even ate the slice Roxie dropped.
Most of the butter stayed on.
We got all the cat hairs off.

Caramel Corn

A new friend moved next door.
His name is Malcomb.
He lives in the apartment
Above the Bocellis.

Malcomb showed me his truck collection.
He's got some good ones.
We dug a hole in the front yard
With one of the earthmovers.

Malcomb's grandfather is rich.
He invented caramel corn.
Malcomb gave me some.
It tastes really good.

I brought a chunk of it home.
But it stuck in my pants pocket.
Maybe it will come out in the wash.
Some got stuck in my sister's hair.

The Messy Room

Mom always says my room is messy.
But it's not my fault.
My room is too small.
I think it used to be a closet.

I don't have enough space
For all my important stuff.
Yesterday, I brought home some rocks
From the Winchester quarry.

They were on the floor by my bed.
Under my blanket.
I forgot to make my bed.
Mom came in and saw the mess.

She kicked the blanket.
Then she started hopping around.
She was pretty mad.
She didn't break her toe.

Billy got my rock collection.

Chess

My friend Mark is short like me.
We play basketball together,
Up on Poplar Street.
Mark talks most of the time.

Mark said I should join Chess Club.
It's at the library.
Chess is like checkers.
Only people don't think as fast.

The pieces all move different.
The king is old and can't run.
Everyone else tries to protect him.
When the king falls over, you lose.

We had our first match last week.
I lost in three moves.
Chess is harder than checkers,
And sometimes it's faster.

Mark said the girl I played was lucky.

This is my sister in her dance stuff.
See how good her hair grew out.

The Dance Recital

My sister had a dance recital today.
Mom said I had to go.
My sister's name is Roxana,
But we all call her Roxie.

Mom made her a nice costume.
It was all shiny and frilly.
She's not doing the tutu stuff.
She's doing the tap dancing.

Some of the show was pretty funny.
One really little kid stopped in the middle.
Part of her costume came off.
Her mom came out to get her.

My sister danced really good.
She even got a solo
When everyone else danced off.
It was a surprise solo.

I liked the costumes.
The little pigs and the mice were best.
We clapped for everybody.
I ate a lot of cookies.

Baseball Cards

There is a great baseball card store
On the corner of Montvale and Main Street.
They also sell comic books
And lots of penny candies.

When I don't go to the movies,
I spend my allowance there.
He has a place in the back
Where we trade comics and cards.

Billy's favorite team is the Indians.
He likes the name and uniforms.
I trade him for the Red Sox.
We both hate the Yankees.

We draw stuff on the Yankee cards
And put them in our bike spokes.
They make a neat noise,
Like when you eat too many beans.

The Golf Course

Billy and I went to Unicorn today.
They have some bad golfers there.
We climbed over the back fence
And collected balls in the woods.

After we filled up Billy's bucket,
We hid out by the eighth tee.
When the players came by
We sold them balls, cheap.

The maintenance guy doesn't like us.
He chased us with a big rake.
We had to run through the woods
And hop back over the fence.

I ripped my school pants.
And Billy lost his bucket.
But we made $1.25.
We bought some new comics and candy.

The Gravel Pit

Last Saturday morning
Billy and I were watching Hopalong Cassidy.
Hoppy was in an old gravel pit
Like the one down by Montvale.

We decided to play Cowboys
Down at our gravel pit.
We were climbing on the chute
And in the abandoned building.

A policeman drove up
And said we were under arrest.
He said we were trespassing
And the building was dangerous.

He knew both our names.
I guess we're pretty famous.
We got a ride in the police car,
But we didn't have to go to jail.

The Farm

Saturday, we went on a Cub Scout trip.
We stayed overnight at a farm.
Everybody brought sleeping bags.
We slept on hay in the barn.

They had chickens and pigs.
We collected eggs from the chickens.
They're not as clean as Mom's.
We had some for breakfast.

We got to ride a horse,
And milked some cows.
I accidentally squirted Billy.
He fell in some meadow muffins.

Billy smelled pretty bad.
Mr. Blaisdell hosed him down.
Billy put an egg in my sleeping bag.
Mom found it on Tuesday. It was broken.

The Black Eye

Billy and I like to play step ball.
You throw a ball off the step
And get hits like baseball.
Last week I hit myself in the eye.

I threw it really hard.
It came back right at me.
It made my vision all fuzzy.
My right eye swelled up good.

I am seeing a lot better,
But I have a black eye.
Actually, it's green and yellow.
All the kids laugh at me.

Butchy says it improved my looks.
Snobby Donna calls me Cyclops.
She says he's a famous monster.
Becky gave me a cookie.

Becky is nice.
If they make us do dancing again,
Maybe I will ask her.
Maybe I won't be too short.

Memorial Day

Warren and I sang at school last Friday.
It was the Memorial Day assembly.
A whole bunch of veterans were invited.
Most of them were really old.

Some came in wheel chairs and on crutches.
They only wore parts of their uniforms, like hats.
I don't think they could fit in the other parts.
All the veterans got little flowers.

Dad played the piano to accompany us.
We sang "My Buddy," "White Cliffs"
And "Coming in on a Wing and a Prayer."
We thought our singing made them cry.

Afterwards, they said we didn't sing bad.
The songs brought back old memories.
They said they were the lucky ones
And that they missed their friends.

Dad marched in the parade today.
Some of the others rode in cars.
At the cemetery they played taps on the bugle.
I'm glad Dad was a lucky one.

Billy's Puppy

Billy's puppy was a mistake.
Mrs. Beaton said some bad dog
Got into her backyard,
And all of a sudden, puppies.

She gave them away last month.
We have three cats,
So no puppies for us.
But Billy got one.

He is funny looking,
Brown and white and squiggly.
He likes to lap your face,
And he tinkled in my lap once.

Billy named him Tipper.
His mom and dad are still deciding
Who takes care of Tipper.
I'm guessing the mom.

Tipper gets in a lot of trouble.
Yesterday, he ate part of Billy's sneaker.
The shoelace came out today
On their living room rug.

Junior Choir

I sing in the junior choir.
I like singing the hymns.
We get to wear red robes
And look really official.

The robes are good to cover you up
If you spill punch on your shirt.
One time I forgot to wear socks;
They didn't hide that.

We go down a hidden passageway
To change into our robes.
Only official people, like me,
Are supposed to use it.

When we sing our solos
They collect all the money.
They do that before the sermon,
When everyone is still awake.

The Soda Fountain

After church is over,
The junior choir kids
All walk up to Middlesex Drugs.
They have a soda fountain.

My favorites are the frappes
With ice cream in them.
But they are pretty expensive.
I usually get a cherry coke.

Wally and Bobby and I go.
We sit at the counter.
The girls go there too.
Wally has a crush on Mimi.

We tease him a lot.
We sing the Do, Re, Mi song.
But we sing Mi, Mi, Mi a lot.
Wally gets all red.

Mimi gets all red too.
Wally finally bought her a soda.
They sat together
At one of the regular tables.

They're probably going to get married.

The Last Day of School

I don't know why we had school today.
We didn't do anything.
Everybody just stared out the window
And waited for the bell to ring.

The teachers let us run around
And didn't get mad at stuff.
Recess was extra long
And we didn't have any books.

Butchy, Billy and I played cards,
And rock, paper and scissors.
Butchy is two years older.
He gives a really hard noogie.

I think Butchy cheats,
But no one argues with him.
Butchy says he is dropping out
As soon as possible.

He says he is tired of the fourth grade.
I think he'll pass this year.
Miss Baker wished him good luck,
And she seemed pretty happy.

York Beach

We go to York Beach in the summer.
It has a great playground.
I build sandcastles
And play in the waves.

We tried to fly a kite.
Dad made it from old newspapers
And sticks and a necktie.
It wouldn't fly.

So instead we went in the surf.
The water was very cold,
But I kind of liked it.
Mom said it made me hyper.

Dad would only go in up to his ankles.
His legs were turning blue.
He looked like he needed help,
So I splashed him.

He chased me down the beach,
But he runs pretty slow
On blue ankles.
Mom brought him a towel.

Later, I was building a sandcastle.
Dad snuck up behind me
And dumped water down my back.
I got even during his nap.

It's good I can run fast.

My aunt says York Beach water is a test of character.
Dad says I'm enough of a character for all of us.

My New Bat

Sometimes I help Stewart deliver newspapers.
Especially on Sunday with the big papers.
He has a flat wagon. We pile it high.
We take turns pulling and delivering.

One day a guy in a truck came with prizes.
He wanted us to sign up new subscriptions.
I went to a lot of houses
And told them what a great paper it was.

I only read the funnies and some sports,
But Grandpa always reads the obituaries,
And Dad does the crossword puzzles.
There must be other good stuff.

I signed up nine subscriptions.
The guy said I needed ten for a new bat.
He said he was leaving in ten minutes.
I ran off to sign up one more.

When I came back, the truck was gone.
But the Eddie Mathews bat was on the grass.
I left the subscription where the bat was.
Sometimes people are pretty nice.

Andover

Sometimes I play with George.
He's the minister's son.
He lives in a parsonage.
We go on trips together.

One time we went to Belmont
To visit my grandparents.
Boy, were they surprised.
My dad came to pick us up.

Everyone thought it was pretty funny.

This year George said "let's go to Andover."
He said we could set a new record.
We didn't know anyone there,
But it sounded like a nice place.

We probably should have turned around
When we got to Reading.
But George wanted a new record.
So we kept walking.

Andover wasn't very exciting.
I borrowed a dime and called Dad.
Dad kept saying, "Andover? Andover?"
I told him it was near Reading.

Nobody appreciated our new record.

The Pool

Yesterday, Billy, Drooley and I went to the pool.
It was really crowded.
They make you shower first.
And wear a metal tag on your ankle.

Kids were running everywhere.
I cannonballed Snobby Donna.
I'm swimming pretty good now.
I even went on the diving board.

The water was really cold,
Except in some spots
Where it gets really warm,
Mostly at the shallow end.

The lifeguard said we couldn't cannonball.
Drooley's suit came off when he dove.
Billy threw it over the fence.
Drooley was really mad.

The lifeguard said we had to leave.
She gave Drooley a towel,
'Cause his suit landed in poison ivy
And nobody would go get it.

Poison Ivy

My cousin Lois is pretty nice.
She's kind of a tomboy.
She likes playing in the dirt,
And the brook and woods.

Last weekend, we were out back
In the woods behind her house.
She was in a bunch of poison ivy.
I knew about it from Cub Scouts.

She said she plays in it all the time.
She isn't allergic to it.
She rubbed it on herself.
I stayed away from it.

Yesterday, Mom said Lois was sick.
She has a rash all over her.
I don't think poison ivy cares
If you're not allergic.

This is my house.
The picture was taken before Dad and I fixed the trellis.

Fixing the Trellis

Dad and I fixed the trellis today.
We just use two tools to fix stuff.
Dad says a hammer and screwdriver
Are all you need to fix almost anything.

All the wood pieces were coming apart.
Maybe because Billy and I climbed on it.
I didn't mention that part to Dad.
I think it was already old and rickety.

At first we made a lot of progress.
Dad and I hammered the pieces together.
That part looked pretty straight.
But the other pieces got loose.

The more we hammered, the more got loose.
Pretty soon we had a big pile of trellis.
Dad said he thought the house looked better.
The trellis was too busy there.

We put the trellis in the basement.
Dad said maybe we'd fix it later.
I think I'm getting good with the hammer.
I hope we fix more stuff soon.

Bare Hill Observatory

Last week, Billy and I
Went up to Bare Hill Observatory.
We were playing Indian scouts
And sneaking through the woods.

Just behind the tower
We saw two big kids.
They were on a blanket
In the pine grove.

They were playing kissy face
Like you see in the movies.
They were missing clothes.
Then Billy stepped on a stick.

We ran back down the hill.
Nobody chased us.
Girls look a lot different
When they get older.

We've been to the observatory
Three times this week.
But nobody is there.
I guess they got cold.

The Chicken Business

Last month, George started a chicken business.
He made me his assistant.
It didn't work out so good.
Pretty soon, the chickens stopped laying.

George was inspecting the rooster
To see about the problem.
The rooster didn't like it much;
He pecked George a good one on the cheek.

George was really, really mad.
He was bleeding pretty good.
After the band-aids, he said no more eggs.
We would take orders for fresh chickens.

We got orders for twelve chickens.
George wanted to start with the rooster,
But we couldn't catch him. He was quick.
We finally caught a regular chicken.

George said I should hold its feet tight,
And put the head on this old stump.
Whack! I had blood all over me.
The chicken ran everywhere without a head.

I resigned as George's assistant.
I didn't want to chase headless chickens,
Or get pecked by angry roosters.
Delivering newspapers is easier.

Cigarettes

I smoked a cigarette once.
Behind McIntyre's cellar.
Billy got them from his brother.
I don't think his brother knew.

They made me dizzy
And I coughed a lot.
Then my eyes started itching
And I threw up.

I tried to sneak back to my room,
But Mom smelled the smoke.
My stomach hurt a lot.
She gave me Castor Oil.

Then Mrs. McIntyre called.
She said we almost started a fire
Down behind her cellar.
Mom said, "Wait 'til your father gets home."

Dad was even madder than Mom.
I got paddled good.
Billy and his brother both got paddled.
Cigarettes are bad for your health.

The back of the McIntyre's house.
Stewart says his mom is still mad about the cigarettes.
I try not to bring it up.

The Swamp

We went to the swamp today.
Some people use it as a dump.
We found part of a car,
And somebody's sofa.

Sometimes we see animals there.
There are muskrats and foxes.
I also saw a deer and a pheasant once.
There are a lot of snakes.

Billy put a snake down my shirt.
It went all the way to my pants.
I jumped around a lot
And took off all my clothes.

It was just a little garden snake.
I pushed Billy into the muck.
He couldn't catch me.
His sneakers were all swampy.

Billy didn't smell so good.
He shouldn't have done the snake thing.
We called a truce.
Billy's mom hates the swamp.

David

David lives down on Lincoln Street.
I met him at school this year.
Sometimes we play at my house.
We never go to his apartment.

Last month we played all day,
Out on my front porch.
We got out chairs and blankets
And made tents out of them.

Last week Mom got a call.
She said David has polio.
David is in the hospital.
We can't play anymore.

Mom called Dr. Andersen about me.
But everything is okay so far.
Mom says I can't go to the pool
At least until next summer.

I think polio is pretty bad,
Mom and Dad seem worried.
They said David moved away.
He lives in an iron lung now.

Uncle Edwin

My cousin Dick and I went to Maine last week,
With Aunt Ginny and Uncle Wally.
Our family is from Prospect Ferry.
We visited with Uncle Edwin.

Uncle Edwin works in the paper mill.
He lives with his mother. They have an outhouse.
Dick and I went to Bucksport with him in his pick-up.
He was going to buy a new truck.

He told me to hold his paper bag.
He said we could look inside.
It was filled with a bunch of money.
Edwin doesn't trust the banks.

After we came back with the new truck,
Edwin shot a deer from the back porch.
We had venison for dinner.
Deer should stay out of Uncle Edwin's yard.

Smelly Feet

Last night we evacuated the living room.
Dad came home really tired
And fell asleep on the couch.
His feet were really smelly.

We tried putting a blanket on him,
But that didn't work.
Then Mom opened the windows,
And put out some Air-Wick.

We all went upstairs, even Mom,
And played in our rooms.
Even the cats came upstairs.
Mom says Dad needs new shoes.

Billy's swamp sneakers smelled bad, too.
His mom threw them out.
Maybe Dad was working in a swamp.
He says it's a jungle out there.

This is my second fish;
I caught him at White Lake.
He was a big one.
He looks smaller in the picture.
(I think they shrink when they get out of the water.)

Fishing

Yesterday we went fishing,
Over at Dike's Pond.
Dad made me a pole
From a stick and string.

He said he would read
While I fished.
We used a dandelion for bait.
I didn't catch anything.

Then we tried a piece of bread.
It got all mushy
And fell off the hook.
I didn't catch anything.

Dad was still reading,
So I tried a piece of ham
From a sandwich in the trash.
I caught a round, orange fish.

Dad was really surprised.
It flopped around a lot,
And then fell back into the water.
I didn't want to eat it, anyway.

Camping

We go camping for vacations.
Billy says it's 'cause Dad is cheap.
Last year, I learned to swim.
I'm happy I know how to swim.

This year we went to Cape Cod.
Dad pitched the tent and got us set up,
Then he went back to Stoneham.
He had to work for the week.

Dad pitched the tent in a creek bed.
It rained and rained and rained.
Stuff in our tent was floating.
A brook ran under our cots.

Dad had the car so we couldn't move.
I lost a sneaker. Roxie lost her socks.
We all walked around in our bare feet
With our pants rolled up.

It rained a lot. The whole week.
The other campers helped us out.
We sat on the picnic table a lot.
Mom was really mad at Dad.

When Dad came back on Friday,
Mom and Dad went to have a talk.
I couldn't hear what they were saying,
But Mom did most of the talking.

Mom and Dad were happier
After it stopped raining,
Until Mom found a little snake
In her sleeping bag.

Our vacation was shorter than usual.
Mom said she needed a rest.
I hope Roxie learns to swim
Before our next camping trip.

Short Cuts

When we go on vacation,
Dad doesn't like the highways.
He says we should see the country.
He likes to explore.

When we were in Canada,
Dad decided to take a short cut.
The roads kept getting smaller.
Then they had grass in the middle.

After we turned around,
We ran out of gas.
It was dark when Dad came back.
We slept in the car.

Then we got lost again.
Dad started hitting the dashboard.
We took the highway home.
We had seen enough country.

Now when Dad talks about taking a short cut,
We all vote for the highway.
Sometimes our votes don't count.
But Mom doesn't like short cuts either.

Her vote seems to count.

Tipper

Billy's dog Tipper is a lot of fun.
He goes on walks with us and chases things.
Sometimes we go to the swamp.
Tipper likes the water.

When Tipper gets wet, he smells bad.
Swamp water is the worst.
Billy's mom doesn't like the swamp.
She gets mad when we take Tipper.

Tipper is easy to feed.
He eats everything, including bad stuff.
One day he ate some really bad stuff
And threw up in Billy's car.

Nobody used the car for a week.
Tipper should be more careful
About what he eats.
I don't let Tipper lap my face anymore.

Car Games

When we take long trips in the car,
We make up games to play.
Dad does this to take our minds off the trip.
And to stop our fighting.

I don't like Who Talks First.
Dad and Mom like that one a lot.
I always lose that game.
They just do it to keep us quiet.

I like the gas station game.
I almost always win that one.
Too bad we don't have good prizes.
The highways are bad for that game.

Dad makes up a lot of new games.
And then changes the rules if he's losing.
Pretty soon we get tired and fall asleep.
And Dad tells us he won.

I think we need written rules.

Mom and Dad and Roxie at Mount Jello.
I took this with my new Brownie.

Old Newspapers

Stewart and I collected newspapers today.
People are happy to get rid of them.
We found a basement loaded with them.
We get 60 cents for every hundred pounds.

We haul them across town to the junk man.
We use Stewart's flat bed wagon.
They have to be neatly stacked,
And they can't be wet.

One day we got caught in the rain.
We had a really big stack.
The load got too heavy to pull,
And we knew the guy wouldn't take them.

We were very wet and tired.
So we left them by the fire station.
We figured this was an emergency.
They're good at dealing with emergencies.

It didn't rain today, though.
Stewart and I made $1.20 each.
The junk man was very pleased.
We didn't go by the fire station.

School

Most of the time, I like school.
But I don't tell anyone.
I like learning new stuff,
And the cookies at recess.

At recess we play fun games,
Like Dodge Ball and Capture the Flag.
I'm good at Dodge Ball
Because I'm little.

Mr. Mullins has pencil erasers.
He keeps them in his pocket.
When kids are bad,
They get hit with them.

He got Billy with one
All the way across the room.
He's pretty funny.
I only got hit once.

I always bring my lunch.
My mom sends sandwiches and fruit.
I trade the fruit to Becky for cookies.
Becky's not a smart trader.

I wish Becky collected baseball cards.

Campsite Toilets

I don't like the toilets when we go camping.
They're like Uncle Edwin's outhouse, only bigger.
I worry about falling through the seat.
They make the opening too big for kids.

Grown-ups don't have to worry as much;
They can cover the whole seat easy.
But kids have to balance on the edge,
And some of the holes are pretty deep.

Last night I had to go really bad,
So I took the flashlight and walked to the toilet.
I was sitting on the edge and lost my balance.
I might have been playing with the flashlight.

The flashlight fell down into the hole.
It sank slowly and the light shined up for a while.
It was a pretty horrible death.
In the dark, I knocked our toilet paper in the hole, too.

I used some leaves from a bush.
I hope they weren't poison ivy.
I stubbed my toe twice walking back.
It was really dark and scary.

In the morning, Dad was looking for the toilet paper.
I told him the flashlight was in the hole.
He was more upset about the toilet paper.
We used *Time* magazine until Dad went to the store.

My Dad's Garden

This summer, Dad tried to grow corn.
He dug up part of our backyard
And put up a little fence.
It came up to my knees.

Dad said not to play in the garden.
He was growing corn and beans.
The fence was to keep out critters.
They must be really little ones.

Not much grew except weeds.
One day a woodchuck was inside the fence.
It was eating Dad's weeds.
It hopped over the fence and left.

By August the garden looked like the yard,
Except the weeds were bigger.
It had some skunk cabbage in it.
Mom bought corn at the store.

She took the little fence
And put it around her violets.
The woodchuck never came back.
At least we didn't grow any turnips.

The Crab Apple Fight

Last week we had a crab apple fight.
Bobby and his brother are troublemakers.
They started throwing crab apples
As Billy and I walked home from school.

Fortunately, it was trash day.
We grabbed a couple of trash lids.
They make good shields.
We got Bobby and his brother good.

Then they got trash lids,
And we called a truce.
Then we threw crab apples
At Allen and Sonny and Drooley.

Then they got trash lids,
And we had another truce.
We left the lids behind Dike's barn,
And all went to play ball on Ted's field.

This week the dogs got in all the trash.
There were papers and stuff everywhere.
The neighbors are all mad at each other.
People with crab apple trees cause a lot of problems.

Robert

Robert is new at school.
He is very quiet and seems sad.
Nobody plays with him.
I think he is lonely.

He offered me a quarter
If I would play with him after school.
He lives up near Maple Street.
It seemed like a good deal.

We played mostly board games.
We had a good time.
I don't think he has a father.
His mom kept checking on us.

I felt bad walking home.
So I walked back to his house.
I told him I didn't need a quarter
To play with him.

His mom invited me to dinner.
She's a really good cook.
We had lamb chops
And mashed potato with gravy.

Toilet Paper

Sometimes I clog up the toilet.
Dad says I use too much toilet paper.
He says three sheets is enough.
Mom says Dad is frugal.

I asked Mom how many sheets she used.
She said maybe six.
I didn't ask Billy,
I know he doesn't use enough.

My little sister is still learning.
She said she pulls off a big wad.
She doesn't count sheets.
Last week she put a kazoo in the toilet.

We had to get a plumber
To get out the kazoo.
Dad is really mad at the toilets.
Maybe I'll cut back to twelve sheets.

The Boy with the Big Head

My mother used to tell me,
"Don't get a big head!"
I never really understood
What she meant.

Then I met Drew,
The boy with the big head,
Who came to the playground
To watch our games.

He wore a brown knit cap,
And had a funny smile.
He knew all our names,
And said, next year, he would play.

I thought he must be smart
To have such a big head.
But he never came to school,
And he never came to play.

Last week I saw his mom
Walking down Hersam Street.
I asked her, "Where is Drew?"
She said he had gone away.

I told my mom
That Drew had gone away.
She said he went with the Angels.
He had water on the brain.

I use ear plugs now,
When I go swimming.
I don't want a big head
And a brown knit cap.

Leaves

I like autumn a lot.
The trees get really pretty,
And when the leaves fall
We can play in them.

Billy's dad rakes them into big piles.
When he gets tired and goes inside
We jump in them
And ride our bikes through them.

Today when Billy jumped in them
He got dog stuff on him.
After that, we jumped in the other pile,
But we smelled it first.

Billy's dad was a little cranky
When he came back out.
Then he stepped in the same dog stuff.
We decided to jump in Mr. Dike's leaves.

My Friend Mark

My friend Mark is Jewish.
His dad is a Rabbi.
I eat dinner at his house sometimes.
They like to play board games.

Mark's whole family is smart.
Except I think they're Democrats.
Otherwise, they're pretty smart.
They go to synagogue.

They said I could go sometime.
Mom said it was okay.
It was different from church
But the front part of the Bible is the same.

A man read from big scrolls,
And they sing some of the speeches
In a foreign language.
I didn't fall asleep.

I like Mark's dad.
He talks to me like a real person.
I like eating at their house,
But sometimes the bread is really stale.

The Proodians

Last night, I stayed with the Proodians.
I stay over with them sometimes.
They live upstairs in an apartment
Down on Hersam Street.

Mrs. Proodian is a good cook.
They are from Armenia.
Mrs. Proodian says not to clean my plate.
She says to leave a bite for the starving Armenians.

I think they had some relatives
Who died from starvation or something.
They call it an old country.
They get sad sometimes to talk about it.

Mr. Proodian plays the violin.
He plays mostly old people music.
Some songs are the same as my piano songs.
They sound better when he plays them.

When I have dinner at home
And Mom serves stuff I don't like
I tell her I want to save it
To send to the starving Armenians.

I don't think she sends it.

Joan's Birthday Party

I went to a birthday party today.
It was for a girl.
Joan is at my school.
She lives down by Montvale.

We play Dodge Ball and Tag at recess.
It was mostly girls at the party.
Just Dicky and Bobby and me for boys.
Billy wasn't invited. She's mad at Billy.

The cake was pretty good,
But we didn't play regular games.
Joan made us all sit in a circle
And we played spin the bottle.

When the bottle pointed to me
They said I had to go in the closet
And do kissy face with Joan.
I was really nervous. I ran home.

The Twenty Dollar Bill

I found a twenty dollar bill last month,
Behind the movie theater and pool hall.
I was really excited bringing it home.
Mom and Dad said I had to turn it in.

We went to the police station to turn it in.
That's where you leave valuable things you find.
They said, if it wasn't claimed in thirty days,
I would be able to keep it.

Last week, I showed Billy where I found it.
When we turned around, a guy was watching.
He was smoking behind the building,
By the back door of the pool hall.

Yesterday, I checked at the police station.
They said someone had just claimed it.
He didn't leave me a reward.
They said it was a guy from the pool hall.

Dad said I did the right thing.
He said he was very proud of me,
Even though I didn't get a reward.
Billy said I was an idiot.

Band Practice

Last month, a band guy came to school.
He wanted us to play instruments.
We get lessons at school
For stuff like trumpets and drums.

Mom said I could learn saxophone.
We have Dad's old saxophone.
Billy is learning the trumpet.
Drooley is playing drums.

When we play, the band guy looks sad.
He says we'll get better.
We can make a lot of noise
But no one plays together.

When I practice at home,
Everyone goes somewhere else.
Billy and I have contests.
So far, he is louder.

Drooley is getting good at drums.
Billy and I think he made a good choice.
We don't want to be around Drooley
When he is blowing on things.

We remember his birthday cake.

Politics

I don't like politics.
Everyone yells and calls each other names.
People make lots of boring speeches.
Then they throw elections to see who wins.

Then they call each other names again.
The teacher says that's okay. That's democracy.
But when I called Wally a name,
I got in trouble.

Dad always gets frustrated at elections.
His candidates never win.
I told him I would help.
I put a sticker on my bike.

We had some democracy at school.
Everyone screamed and yelled at me.
They drew a mustache on my sticker.
I don't think Dad's candidate is going to win.

The Dentist

I went to the dentist yesterday.
He said I had cavities.
I need to brush better,
And eat less candy.

He said I needed fillings.
He wanted to use a big drill
To get all the candy out
And fill the holes with yucky stuff.

He put a black mask on me.
It smelled like old rubber.
I threw up in it.
Then I threw up again.

He didn't fill any cavities.
I don't like the dentist.
And I don't like big drills.
It's bad when throwing up is the best part.

This is us playing ukuleles.
Mom made us get all dressed up.
We got a deal on the shoes.

Thanksgiving Dinner

Mom cooked two turkeys this year.
We had a lot of guests.
Even Aunt Lil came from Connecticut.
There were people and kids everywhere.

Mom made so many vegetables
That she forgot two of them.
She remembered at dessert.
I didn't have to eat the turnip.

I like Thanksgiving dinner.
I put gravy on everything,
Even the cranberry jelly.
It kind of hides the vegetables.

We had a really long prayer.
Aunt May fell asleep.
I think Mom thought she was sick,
But she woke right up again.

They put all the kids out in the kitchen.
That was a lot of fun.
Mom was upset about the peas.
She shouldn't serve peas to kids in the kitchen.

Nemia

Last week, Mom was sick.
The doctor came on Monday.
He said she had a nemia.
She looked very tired.

I don't know what a nemia is,
But my sister probably made her tired.
Dad sure looked worried.
I don't think he knows how to cook.

Nemia sounds pretty bad.
Mom has to eat cabbage and liver.
And she seems very sleepy.
I made Mom some toast with jelly.

Mom got some shots from Dr. Anderson
And now she's feeling better.
That's good news because Dad's a wreck.
I hope we don't eat liver and cabbage all the time.

The Basement Toilet

We have a toilet in the basement.
It's behind the furnace,
Next to the old coal bin,
Up on a wooden platform.

It doesn't have any walls.
Dad says it's for emergencies.
We don't tell guests about it.
My mom and sister won't use it.

We only had one toilet before.
Sometimes Grandpa got stuck in there.
This caused some of the emergencies.
The plumber gave Dad a deal.

I don't think Mom liked the deal.
She still wants a real bathroom.
She says it doesn't even have a light.
Dad put a flashlight by the plunger.

It does get a little scary sometimes.
Especially when the furnace comes on.
A mouse came out of the coal bin yesterday.
He watched me do my business.

White Christmas

This year we had a white Christmas.
It was really white.
The snow came up to my waist.
It looked like in the movie.

Dad shoveled a lot the day before.
I helped some, but I got tired,
So my sister and I built a snowman
And made snow angels.

We went to church Christmas Eve,
But the car got stuck.
We all got out and pushed, even Grammy.
We were late for church.

When we got home
Dad had to shovel the driveway again.
I told Dad not to worry,
Santa's sleigh wouldn't get stuck.

My sister and I woke everyone at 6:00 A.M.
Santa's sleigh didn't get stuck.
We played Christmas carols.
The snow was still falling.

After we opened the presents,
Dad went out to shovel again.
I hit him with a snowball.
I don't think he likes white Christmases.

My Christmas Presents

My Christmas presents started off bad.
I thought Santa's sleigh got stuck in the snow.
All I got in my stocking
Was a banana, an apple and a lump of coal.

The coal was from the cellar.
Santa's budget must have been low.
My tree presents were even worse.
Underwear, socks, handkerchiefs and a necktie.

I was very disappointed.
I decided to eat the apple.
My sister got lots of good stuff.
And she was almost as bad as me.

Then Mom said she forgot,
Santa left one more present.
It was a big one for me.
It was Fort Apache with Rusty and Rin Tin Tin.

Billy and I put it together.
Then we shot all the cavalry
With the rocket launchers
We got in the Rice Krispies boxes.

Fort Apache surrendered with my handkerchief.
The Indians hung Rusty with my necktie.
Billy and I ate Aunt May's candy,
And we used the banana on the snowman.

It turned out to be a pretty good Christmas.
Although Mom made us take the banana off the snowman.

Acknowledgements

The reason this poetry is so good is that my teachers helped me with the spelling and grammar. (Sometimes I didn't listen, 'cause teachers talk kind of funny and I might put kids to sleep if I said everything like the teachers do.)

At least they didn't make me write a bunch of rhymes and use a whole bunch of fancy poetry stuff. Most of the time, when they make us read poetry with fancy stuff in it, I don't know what they're saying.

My teachers are pretty nice and even though this started as extra homework, it turned out kind of fun. Sometimes, like when Billy and I sneak off to go to the quarry, they get upset. They say I exasperate them. I'm not exactly sure what that means, but I think it has something to do with detention.

Most of the time though, I like them a lot. So thank you to Miss Thompson and Miss Baker and Miss Barry and Mister Mullins for helping to make this book so good.